I Can DRAW
Dinosaurs

Cover illustrated by Renée Daily

Interiors illustrated by Yuri Salzman

D0131766

Here's what you need...

You're about to become an artist! Before you start, make sure you have a pencil, a pencil sharpener, an eraser, a felt-tip pen, and one or more of the the different coloring media pictured here. Then, look in the back of the book for your grid pages. They'll help you to follow the special drawing steps. If you need more paper, you can ask a grownup to help you to copy them.

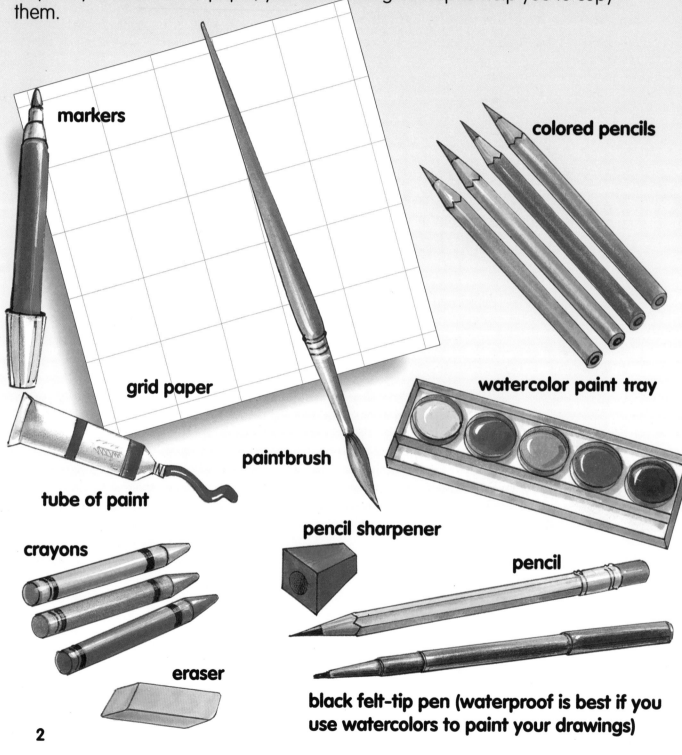

markers

colored pencils

grid paper

watercolor paint tray

paintbrush

tube of paint

pencil sharpener

crayons

pencil

eraser

black felt-tip pen (waterproof is best if you use watercolors to paint your drawings)

And here's what you do!

1 Copy each step-by-step drawing onto your grid paper, noticing where the drawing should touch the lines on your grid. Draw lightly in pencil. Since each new step is shown in blue, you'll always know exactly what to do next.

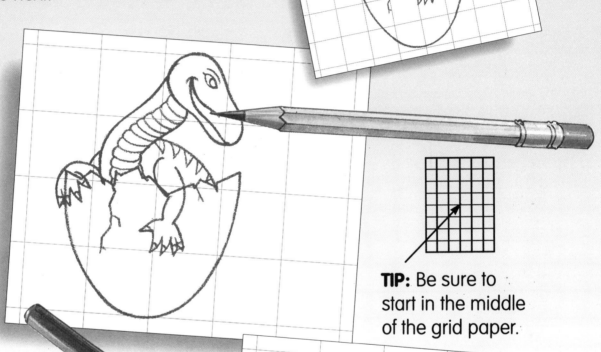

TIP: Be sure to start in the middle of the grid paper.

2 When you've drawn all the steps shown in blue, use your felt-tip pen to trace over the pencil lines you need to keep, then erase all the extra pencil lines.

Now you have a perfect drawing to color any way you'd like! Before you color, you may want to read pages 30 to 32 for some extra coloring tips.

3

Hypselosaurus

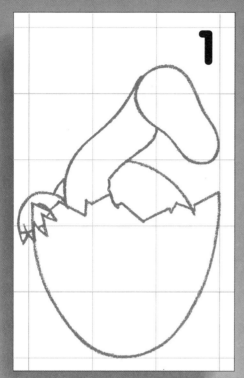

1 Draw half of an oval with a jagged line across the top. This will be the dinosaur egg. Draw a bean shape for the baby dinosaur's head, and curved lines for its neck and body. Add an arm.

2 Add the other arm, stripes, an eye, a nostr and a big, open mouth with lots of pointy teeth

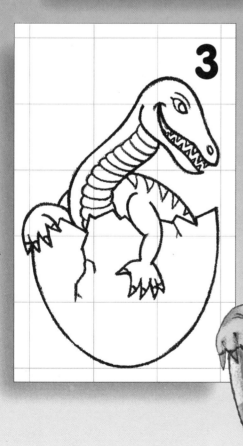

3 Use your felt-tip pen to trace over the pencil lines you want to keep, and erase all the others.

No one really knows what colors dinosaurs were, so you can make up your own patterns and designs for your drawings.

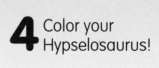

4 Color your Hypselosaurus!

4

Tylosaurus

1 Long, curved lines and small circles make your Tylosaurus' spotted body. Add two flippers.

2 Draw two wavy lines and two more flippers, sharp teeth, an eye, and decorative details on the face.

3 Use your felt-tip pen to trace over the pencil lines you want to keep, and erase all the others.

4 Color your Tylosaurus!

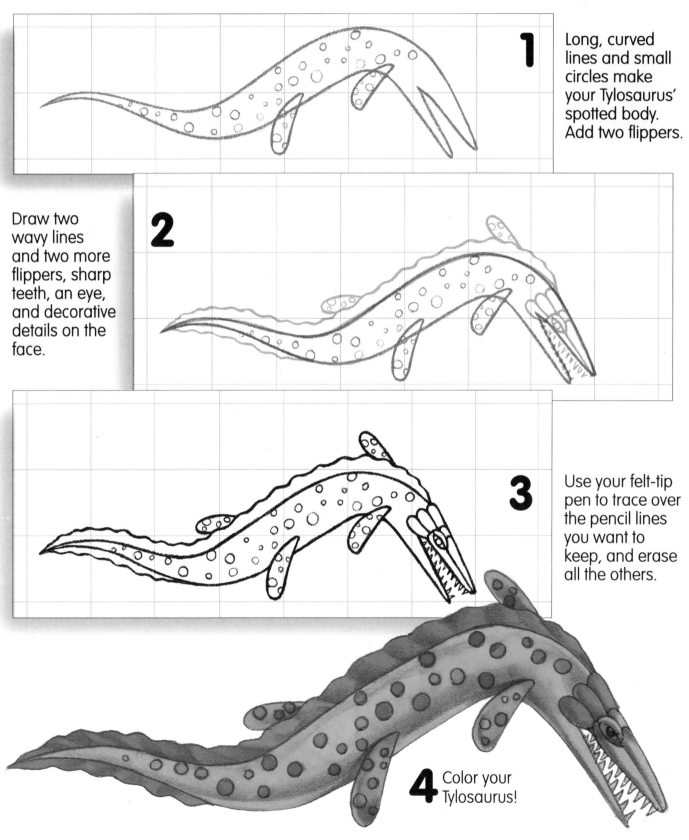

Allosaurus

1 Draw the head and the body.

Use curved lines to draw a tail, thighs, and an upper forearm. Connect the head to the body with more curved lines.

2

3 Finish the legs and the forearms. Add a big, open mouth, an eye, and a nostril.

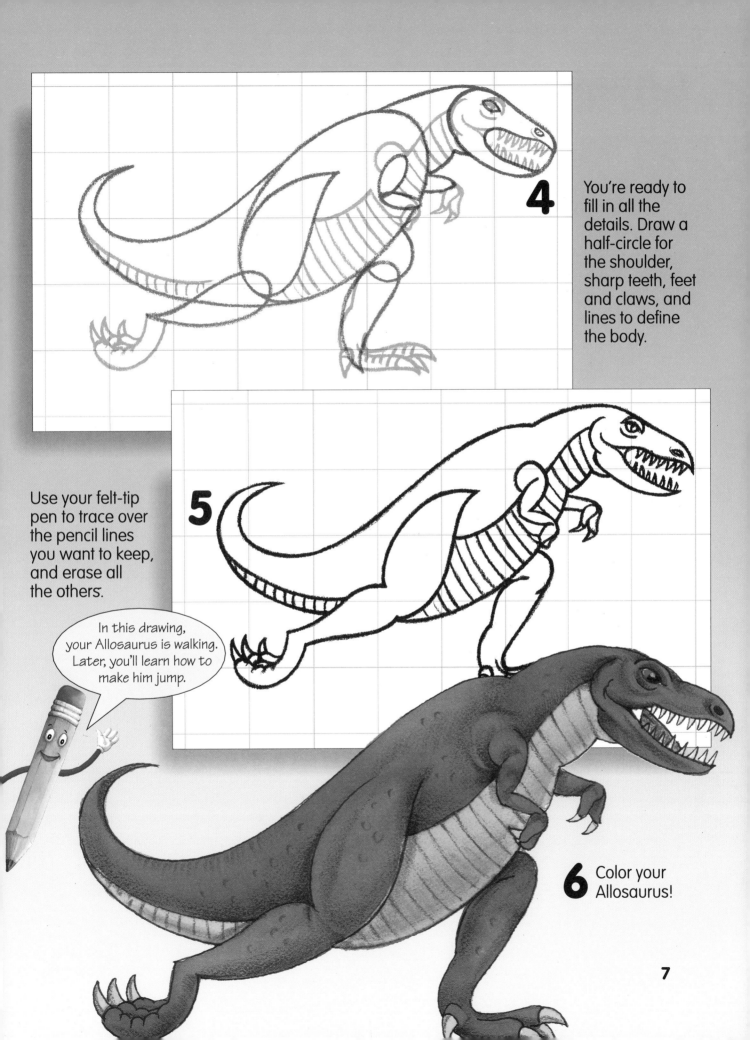

4 You're ready to fill in all the details. Draw a half-circle for the shoulder, sharp teeth, feet and claws, and lines to define the body.

5 Use your felt-tip pen to trace over the pencil lines you want to keep, and erase all the others.

In this drawing, your Allosaurus is walking. Later, you'll learn how to make him jump.

6 Color your Allosaurus!

Iguanadon

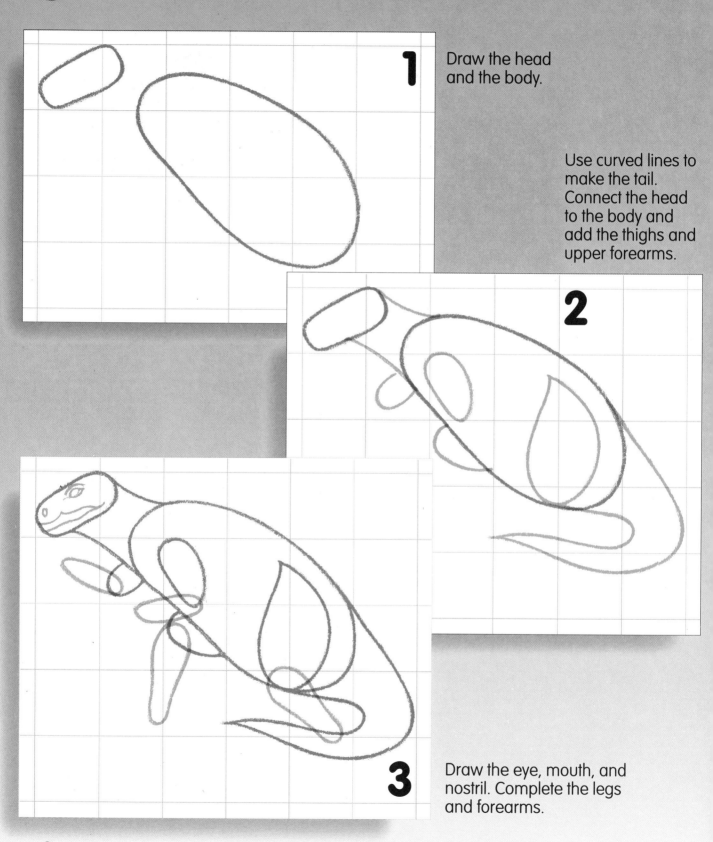

1 Draw the head and the body.

Use curved lines to make the tail. Connect the head to the body and add the thighs and upper forearms.

2

3 Draw the eye, mouth, and nostril. Complete the legs and forearms.

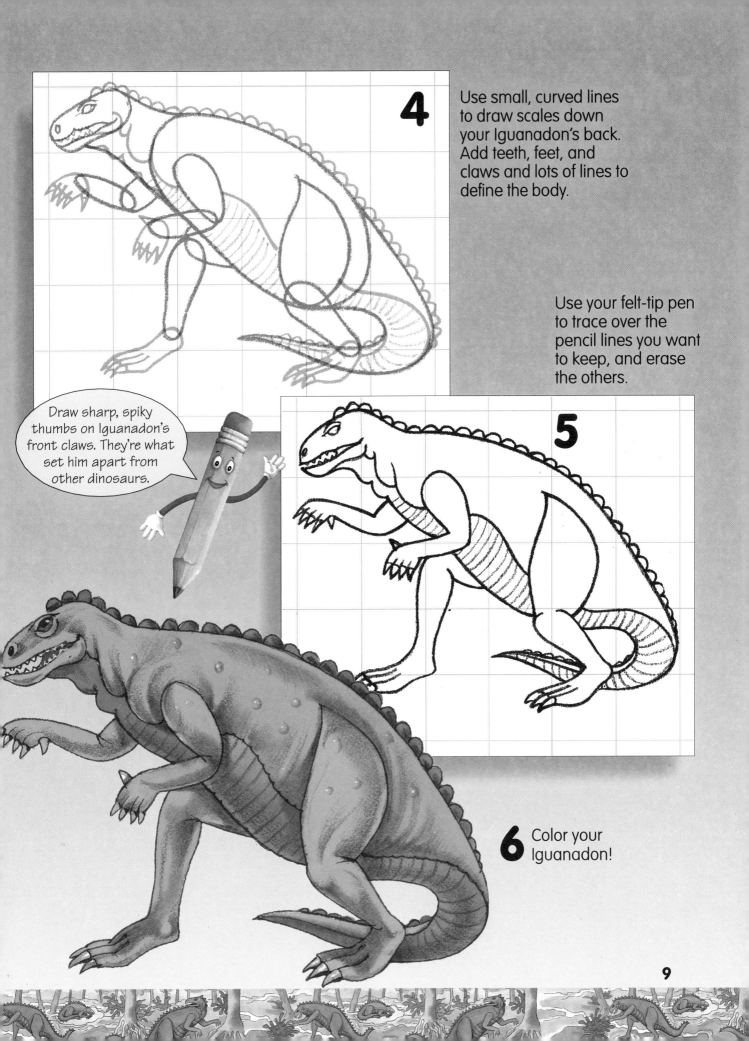

4 Use small, curved lines to draw scales down your Iguanadon's back. Add teeth, feet, and claws and lots of lines to define the body.

Use your felt-tip pen to trace over the pencil lines you want to keep, and erase the others.

5

Draw sharp, spiky thumbs on Iguanadon's front claws. They're what set him apart from other dinosaurs.

6 Color your Iguanadon!

9

Dinosaurs in Action

Use the same kinds of shapes you used to draw your Allosaurus to make him jump! The body, arms, and head stay in the same positions. But look at how the legs are drawn. One leg is stretched out, raising the body high off the ground. The other leg is bent in close to the body.

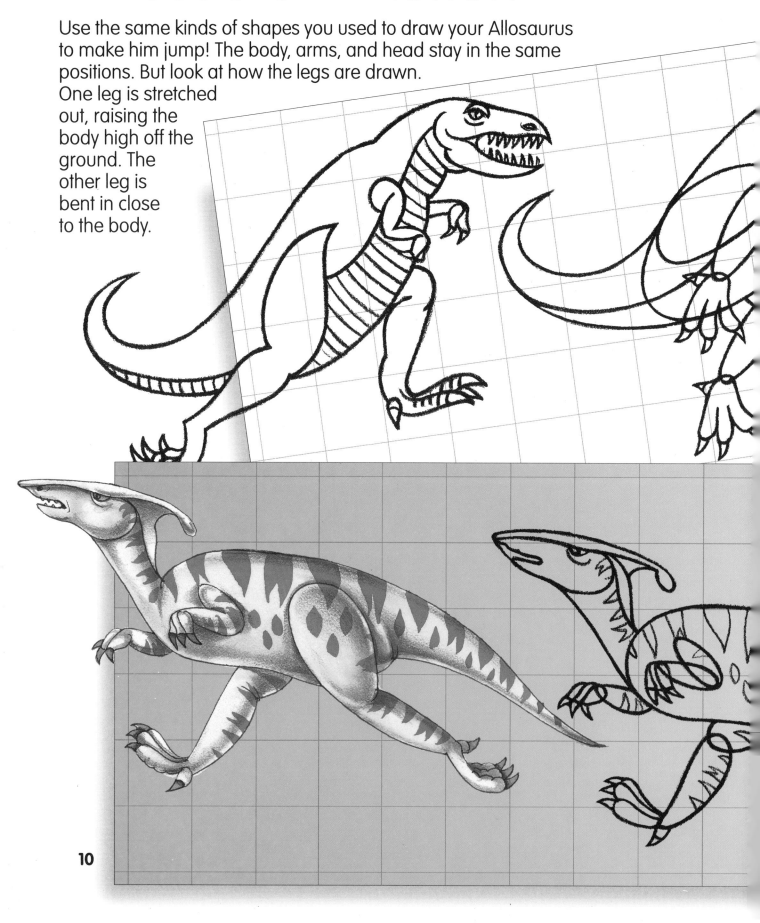

Experiment with different leg positions to make the dinosaurs in this book run and jump!

This Parasaurolophus is shown moving from a walk to a run. Its legs, tail, and neck stretch out, and the body is lower to the ground.

11

Plesiosaurus

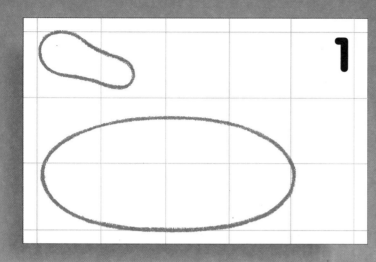

1

Draw an oval for the Plesiosaurus' body and a bean shape for its head.

Use two curved lines to connect the head to the body. Add the tail.

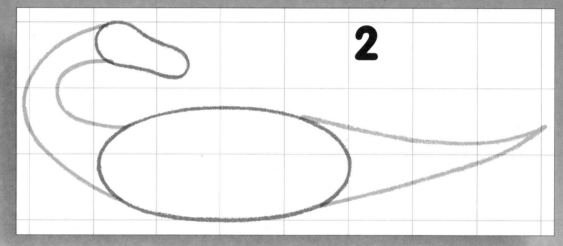

2

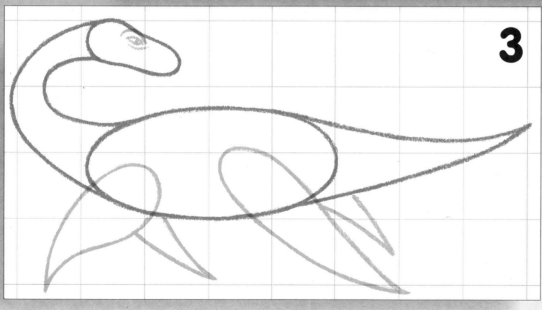

3

More curved lines, joined together, create the flippers. Add an eye.

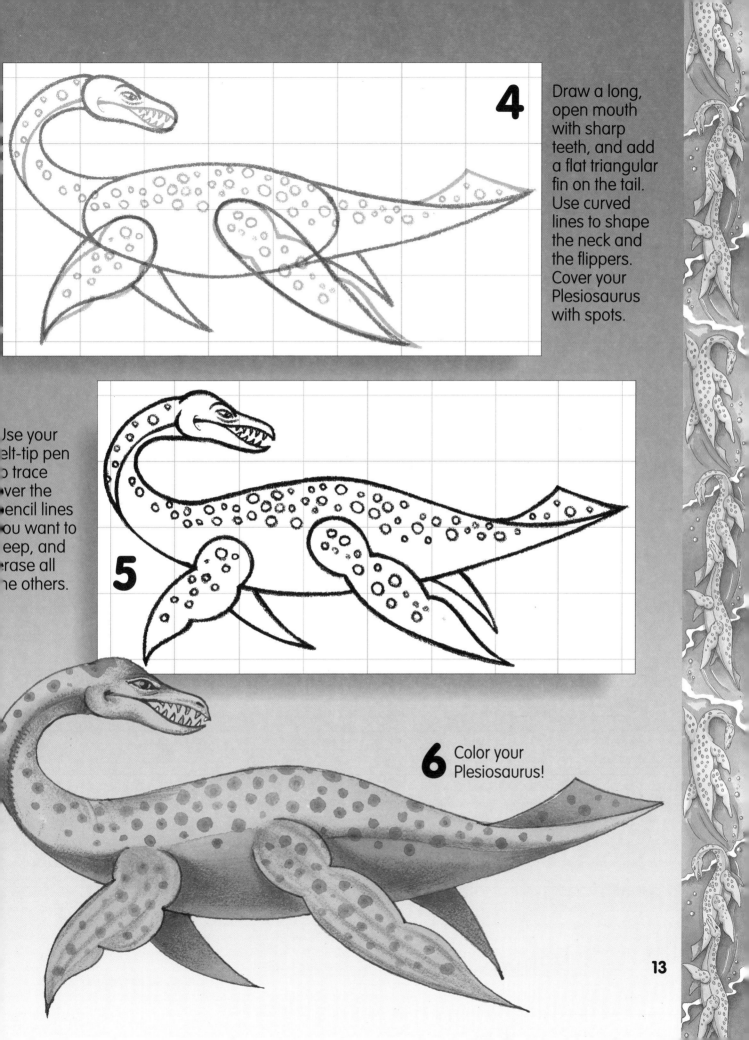

4 Draw a long, open mouth with sharp teeth, and add a flat triangular fin on the tail. Use curved lines to shape the neck and the flippers. Cover your Plesiosaurus with spots.

5 Use your felt-tip pen to trace over the pencil lines you want to keep, and erase all the others.

6 Color your Plesiosaurus!

13

Stegosaurus

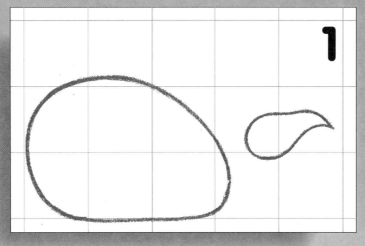

1 Draw the body and the head.

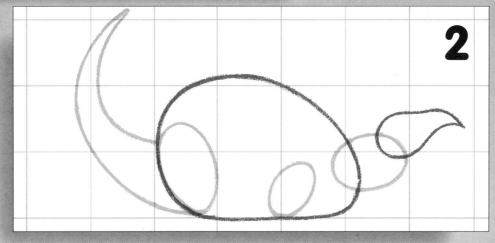

2 Draw ovals for the neck and the tops of the legs. Use curved lines for the tail.

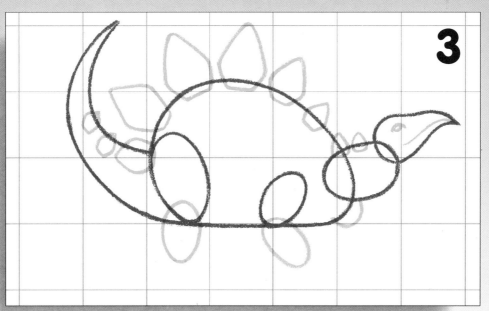

3 Add pointed plates down your Stegosaurus' back, tail, and neck. Draw a mouth and an eye, and finish the legs.

4 Draw the feet and toes. Add sharp spikes to the tail and more plates on the back. Then add details on the body, scales, and head.

Because of the way your Stegosaurus is standing, the left hind leg does not need to be drawn. A few toes are all you see from this angle.

5 Use your felt-tip pen to trace over the pencil lines you want to keep, and erase all the others.

6 Color your Stegosaurus!

plant

volcanos

seaweed

16

Making Backgrounds

You can draw backgrounds using the same kinds of drawing steps you've been using to draw your dinosaurs. These pages show some of the possibilities. Just start with basic shapes, and add the details one step at a time.

Learn to draw Triceratops on pages 26 and 27. ▲

Learn to draw Allosaurus on pages 6 and 7. ▲

Learn to draw Stegosaurus on pages 14 and 15. ▲

Learn to draw Tylosaurus on page 5. ▲

Parasaurolophus

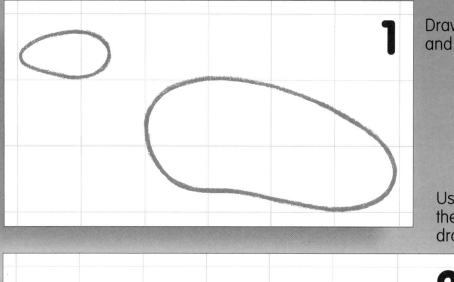

1 Draw the head and the body.

Use curved lines to make the tail and the neck, and draw the tops of the legs.

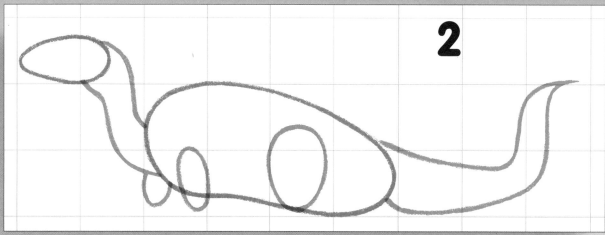

2

Add the eye and an extra line on the neck. Finish the legs.

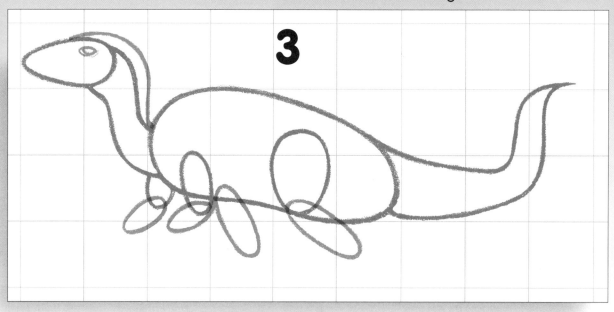

3

18

4 Draw feet and claws. A long crest goes on top of this dinosaur's head. Add body markings.

5 Use your felt-tip pen to trace over the pencil lines you want to keep, and erase all the others.

Turn to page 10 to see how to make your Parasaurolophus run!

6 Color your Parasaurolophus!

Dimetrodon

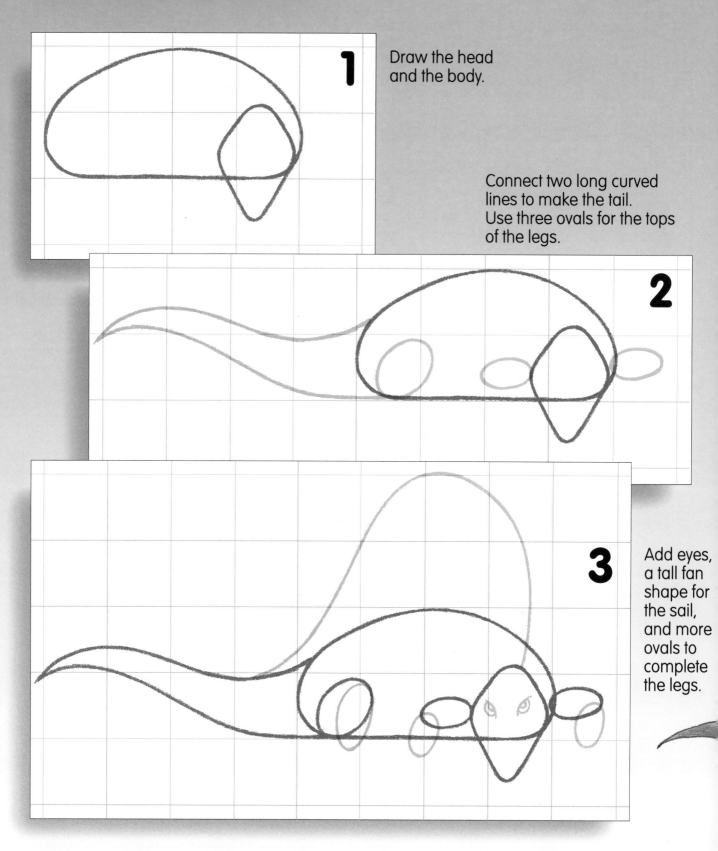

1 Draw the head and the body.

Connect two long curved lines to make the tail. Use three ovals for the tops of the legs.

2

3 Add eyes, a tall fan shape for the sail, and more ovals to complete the legs.

4 Finish your Dimetrodon with details such as feet, a nose, a mouth, round scales, and tall spikes on its sail.

Use your felt-tip pen to trace over the pencil lines you want to keep, and erase all the others.

5

6 Color your Dimetrodon!

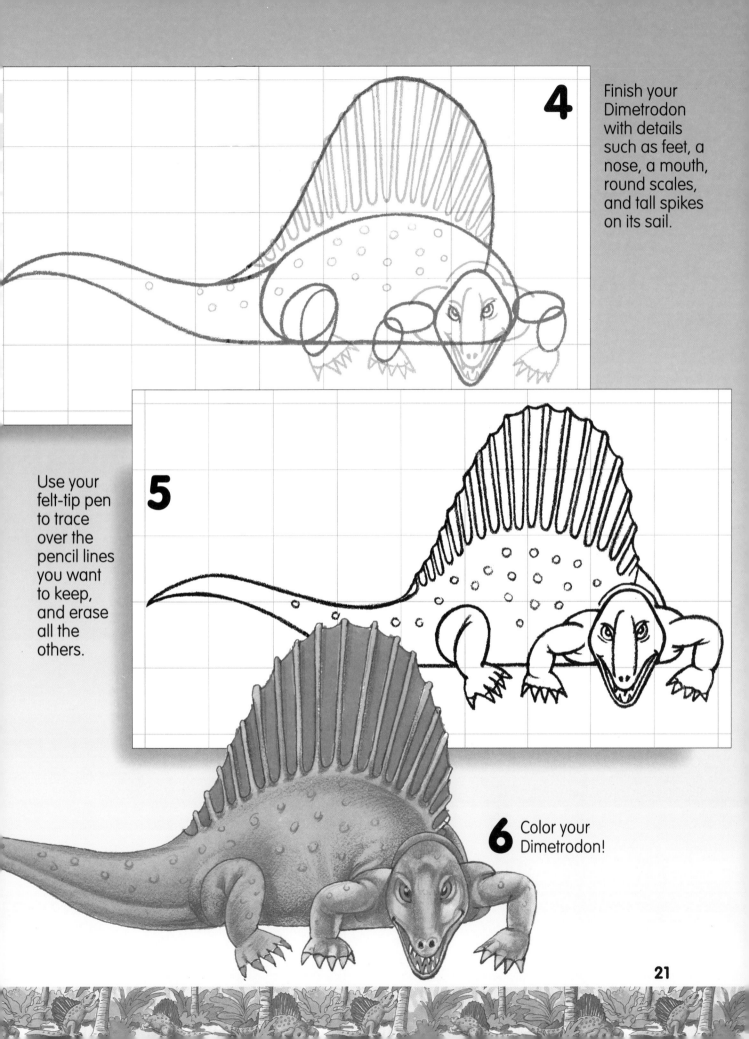

Ankylosaurus

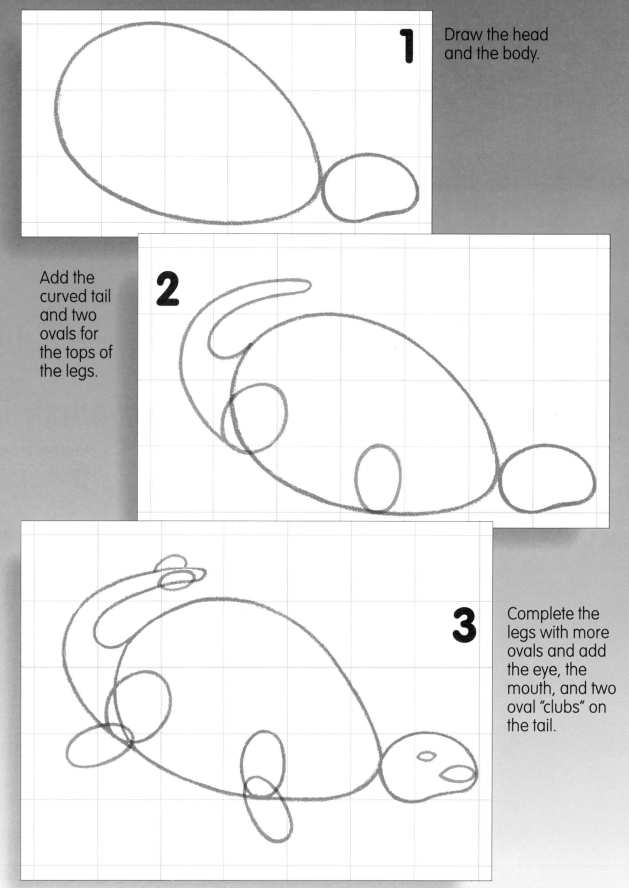

1 Draw the head and the body.

2 Add the curved tail and two ovals for the tops of the legs.

3 Complete the legs with more ovals and add the eye, the mouth, and two oval "clubs" on the tail.

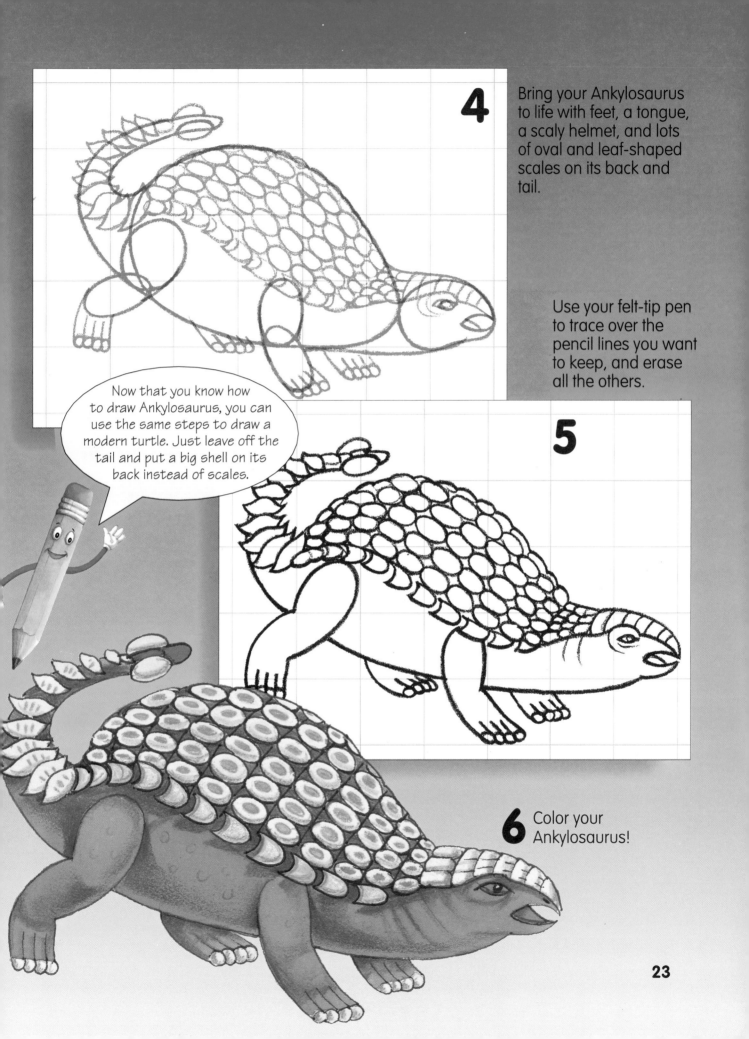

4 Bring your Ankylosaurus to life with feet, a tongue, a scaly helmet, and lots of oval and leaf-shaped scales on its back and tail.

Use your felt-tip pen to trace over the pencil lines you want to keep, and erase all the others.

Now that you know how to draw Ankylosaurus, you can use the same steps to draw a modern turtle. Just leave off the tail and put a big shell on its back instead of scales.

5

6 Color your Ankylosaurus!

cliff

tree

shrub

Putting It All Together

Once you can draw a few dinosaurs and give them backgrounds, you can create a scene. Draw the dinosaurs you have decided to have in your scene, then build a background around them. The dinosaurs in this scene didn't all really live at the same time. You may want to research which prehistoric periods your favorite dinosaurs lived in so that you can put the ones that really walked the earth together in the same scene.

24

Triceratops

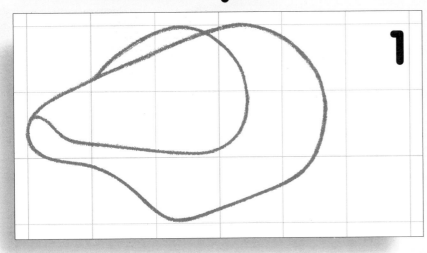

1 Draw overlapping shapes for the head and the body.

Use ovals and curved lines to make the upper legs and the tail.

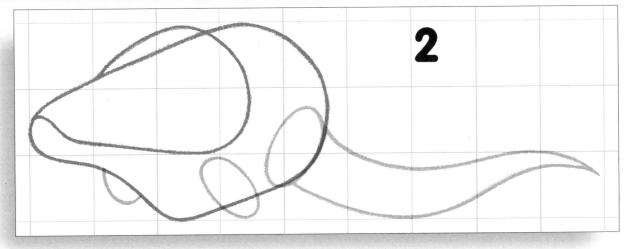

2

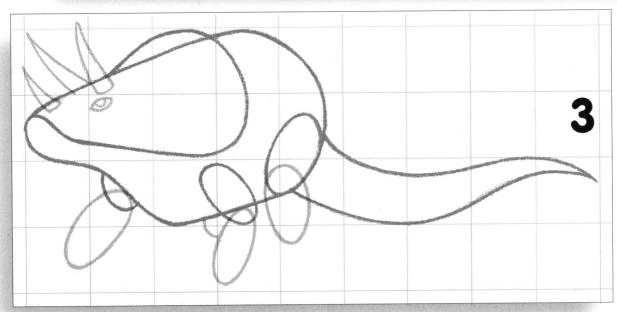

3 Add an eye and horns. Complete the legs.

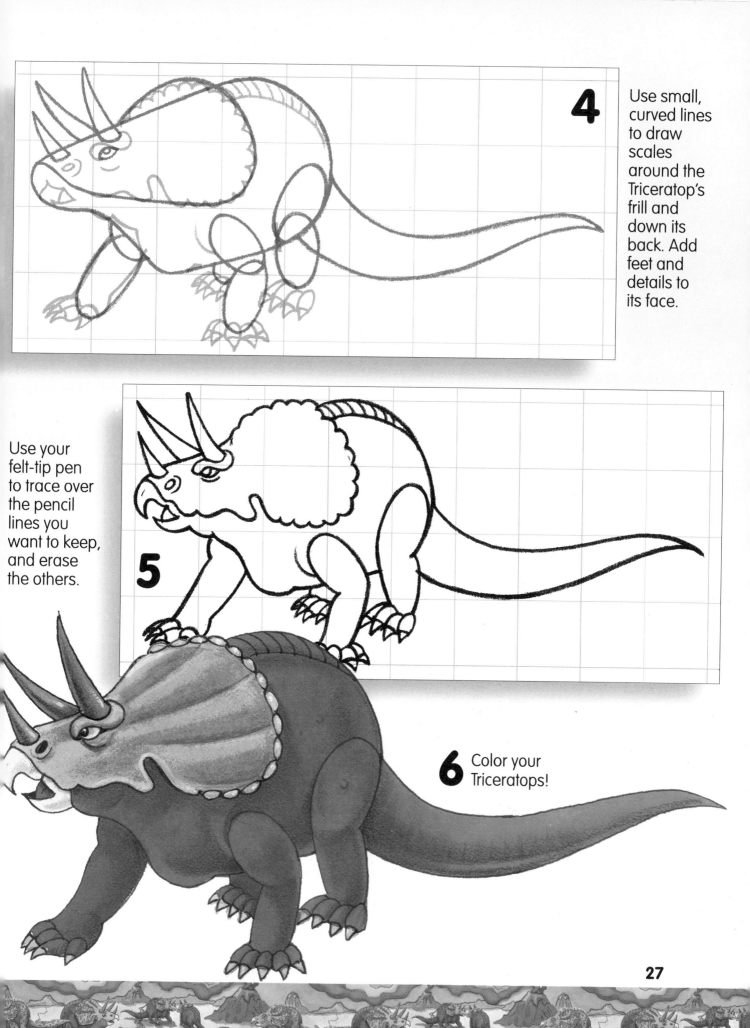

4 Use small, curved lines to draw scales around the Triceratop's frill and down its back. Add feet and details to its face.

Use your felt-tip pen to trace over the pencil lines you want to keep, and erase the others.

5

6 Color your Triceratops!

Diplodocus

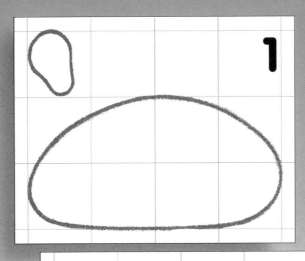

1 Draw the body and the head.

Use long, curved lines for the neck and tail, and draw the tops of the legs.

2

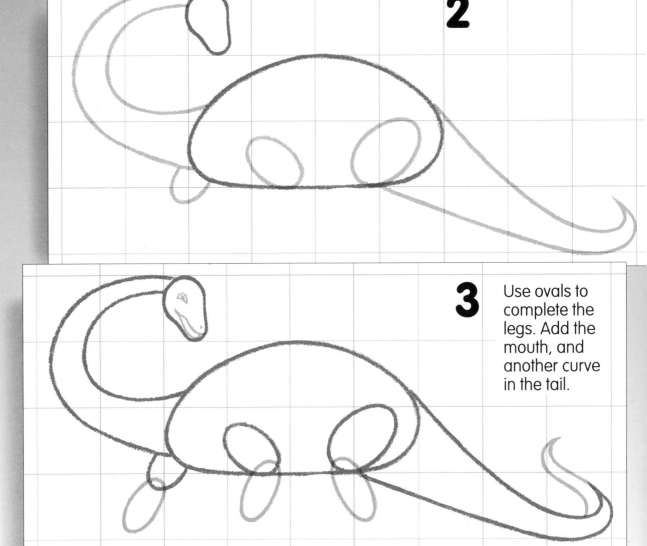

3 Use ovals to complete the legs. Add the mouth, and another curve in the tail.

4 Draw the feet, shoulders, and the end of the tail. Add lines to define the neck and body.

Use your felt-tip pen to trace over the pencil lines you want to keep, and erase all the others.

5

6 Color your Diplodocus!

Coloring Your Drawings

Once you've finished the outlines of your drawings, it's fun to color them in. Use watercolor paints, colored pencils, crayons, markers, or anything else you can think of!

Watercolors are fun to use, but sometimes when two wet paint colors are next to one another, they run together. If you're using watercolors, you might want to let the paint dry after each color you use.

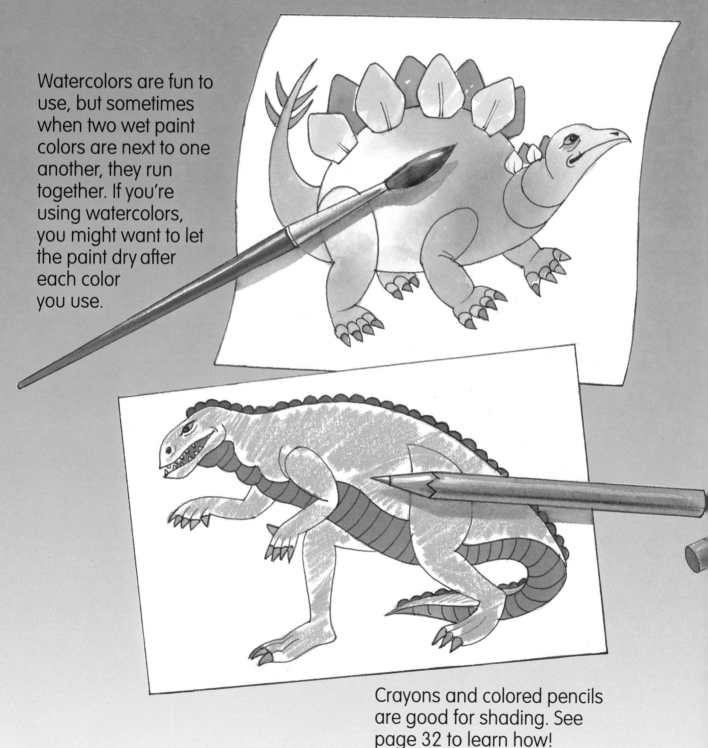

Crayons and colored pencils are good for shading. See page 32 to learn how!

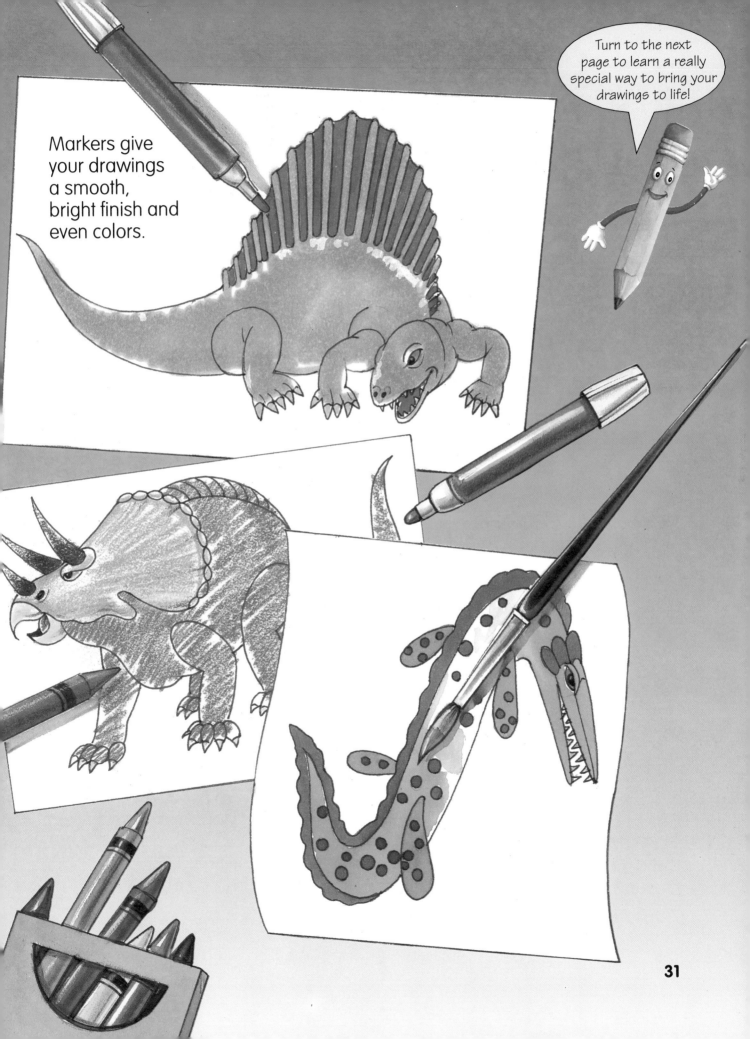

Shading Your Drawings

Shading can add dimension and life to your drawings. Try shading first with a crayon or colored pencil. Make an area of your dinosaur darker where there would be less light on the dinosaur. Then add lighter color where the light would hit the dinosaur, and watch your drawing come to life!

Use these grid pages for your drawings. Make extra copies so you can draw lots of pictures using the special steps in this book!